The 2016 first edition is published by **Aquaterra Publishing**

5 Canons Close
Bishopsteignton
Teignmouth
Devon
TQ14 9RU
Great Britain

www.aquaterrapublishing.co.uk

ISBN 978-0-9927970-1-0

Front cover: Sunset over the sea seen from Bolt Head, near Salcombe, on the south coast of Devon.

Left inset photograph – Bog Asphodel, *Narthecium ossifragum*.
Right inset photograph – Eurasian Otter, *Lutra lutra*.

Front cover flap: A Small Pearl-bordered Fritillery butterfly, *Clossiana selene*.

Back cover: Woodland at the eastern end of Chedder Gorge, Somerset.

Half title page: A Sand Pansy, *Viola tricolor ssp curtisii*, Braunton Burrows National Nature Reserve.

Title page (right): A Dipper, *Cinclus cinclus*, on the East Lyn River, Exmoor National Park.
Inset photograph – Greater Knapweed, *Centaurea scabiosa*.

Text and cover design:
Topics – The Creative Design Partnership,
Exeter, Devon, Great Britain.
www.topicsdesign.co.uk

Printed in China by
PWGS (Singapore) Pte Ltd

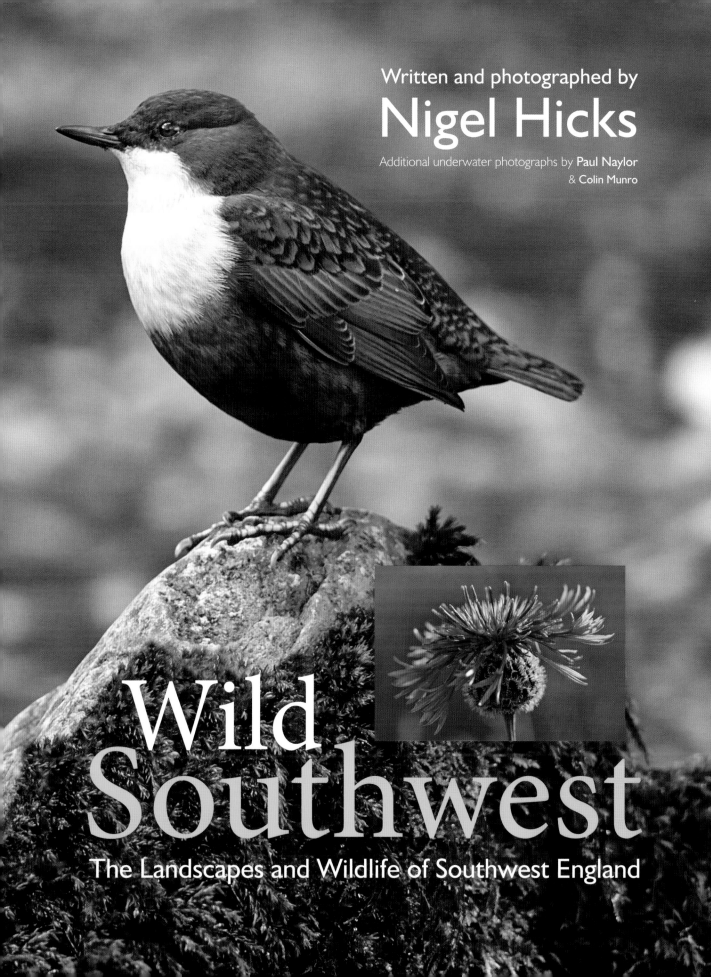

Written and photographed by
Nigel Hicks

Additional underwater photographs by **Paul Naylor**
& Colin Munro

Wild Southwest

The Landscapes and Wildlife of Southwest England

Chalk cliffs tower above the beach at Durdle Door, in the Jurassic Coast World Heritage Site, Dorset.

Introduction

We live in a world today where fast, international travel is easy, where television and the internet give us virtually instantaneous windows onto almost any corner of the globe at any moment of the day or night. It is a world where wildlife and travel documentaries give the impression that extreme, odd and just downright weird environments, wildlife and destinations are actually the norm, though only in exotic far away places, never close to home, in our own back yard. We become ever more fixated on the distant, convinced there is nothing worth seeing in our home area, determined to go to ever greater lengths to reach and experience the extremes, so we can come home and say 'We went there, we saw it.'

Yet sometimes, some of the world's greatest beauty is right on our doorstep. We just have to stop and look around. This, I believe is the case

Left: A Barn Owl, *Tyto alba*.

Above: A stormy autumnal afternoon, shortly before sunset, at Thurlestone, south Devon.

9

Above: A Harvest Mouse, *Micromys minutus*, balances on an ear of wheat.

Below: The magnificent chalk cliffs of the Pinnacles, near Studland, at the eastern end of the Jurassic Coast World Heritage Site, Dorset.

with the southwest of England, that long narrow peninsula stretching from Bristol to the Isles of Scilly, pointing out into the vastness of the Atlantic Ocean. All right, so the southwest does not have lions, tigers, gorillas, meekats or glacier-covered mountains, but nowhere has all those things, and most places don't have any. But what the southwest does have is rugged cliffs and vast beaches, in the west pounded by Atlantic surf, in the east one of the world's most important geological tableaux. Much of the landscape is intensely rural, significant parts of it wild open moors and dense, lush woodlands.

Landscapes vary from high moorland hills, to deep wooded valleys, to coastal dunes and surf-battered cliffs in incredibly short distances, an amazing diversity packed into this one peninsula. Wildlife too, is remarkably varied, ranging from offshore seals, dolphins, sharks and cold water corals (yes, we do have some – they are not just for the tropics!), to more familiar terrestrial wildlife, such as the red deer (Britain's largest land animal), otters, birds of prey, bluebells and weirdly beautiful orchids (again something that is not just for the tropics). It should be remembered that wildlife is not only about animals: the plants are every bit as important.

Wild Southwest aims to introduce some of the best natural landscapes and wildlife that southwest England has to offer, covering the counties of Somerset, Dorset, Devon and Cornwall, and ranging from the reefs and

Above: Primroses, *Primula vulgaris*, a harbinger of spring, in a woodland in Dartmoor National Park, Devon.

sandy seabed beneath the waves to the highest moorland tors. Inevitably, in a book of this size it is impossible to cover absolutely everything, and much of what is here has had to be simplified in the interests of space. So, this is more a taster of what is on offer, introducing many of the most beautiful and important landscapes and wildlife (both plant and animal), as well as some of my own personal favourites. If I have missed out any of your own choices, then I apologise.

The book starts with an introduction to the southwest's landscapes, followed by a summary of some of its plant and animal wildlife. Once the scene is set, we then travel around the region, moving roughly from east to west, starting with the amazing Jurassic Coast and ending with the Isles of Scilly. Along the way we pass through Dorset's heaths and chalk grasslands, Somerset's Mendip and Quantock Hills, as well as its marshy Levels, and on to the wilds of Exmoor and Dartmoor. Inevitably, as we head further west so the coast and sea become increasingly important, though many of the heaths and moors of the far west are also covered.

It is hoped that the text and photography in combination will paint a vivid and inspiring picture of the beauty of southwest England's natural environment and wildlife, demonstrating that there is much that is beautiful, striking, important and very worth protecting close to home. The photography unashamedly aims to show off as visually as possible the dramatic beauty of the southwest's landscapes and wildlife, while the text aims to be both highly informative and entertaining. I hope you enjoy the tour.

Above: A Speckled Wood butterfly, *Pararge aegeria*, in a suburban garden.

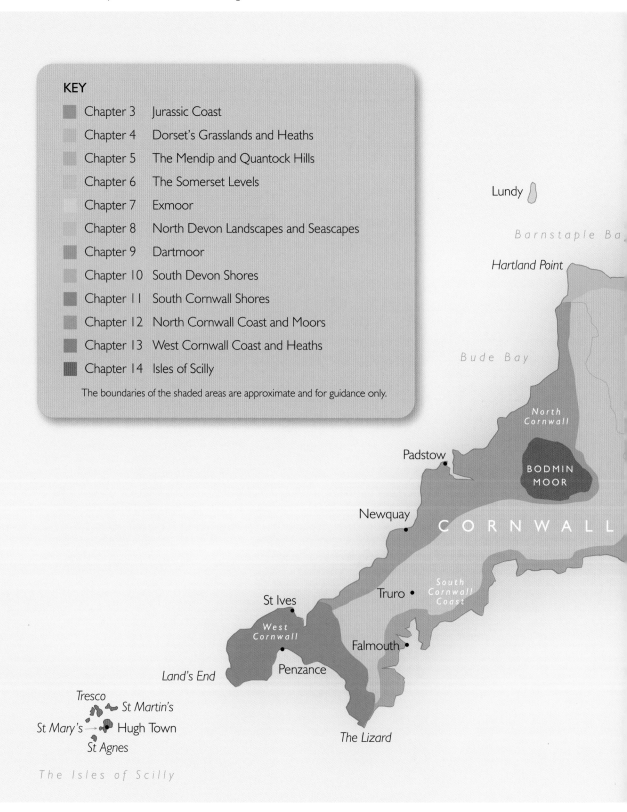

KEY

Chapter 3   Jurassic Coast

Chapter 4   Dorset's Grasslands and Heaths

Chapter 5   The Mendip and Quantock Hills

Chapter 6   The Somerset Levels

Chapter 7   Exmoor

Chapter 8   North Devon Landscapes and Seascapes

Chapter 9   Dartmoor

Chapter 10   South Devon Shores

Chapter 11   South Cornwall Shores

Chapter 12   North Cornwall Coast and Moors

Chapter 13   West Cornwall Coast and Heaths

Chapter 14   Isles of Scilly

The boundaries of the shaded areas are approximate and for guidance only.

Lundy

Barnstaple Ba

Hartland Point

Bude Bay

North Cornwall

Padstow

BODMIN MOOR

Newquay

C O R N W A L L

Truro

South Cornwall Coast

St Ives

West Cornwall

Falmouth

Land's End

Penzance

Tresco

St Martin's

St Mary's → Hugh Town

St Agnes

The Lizard

The Isles of Scilly

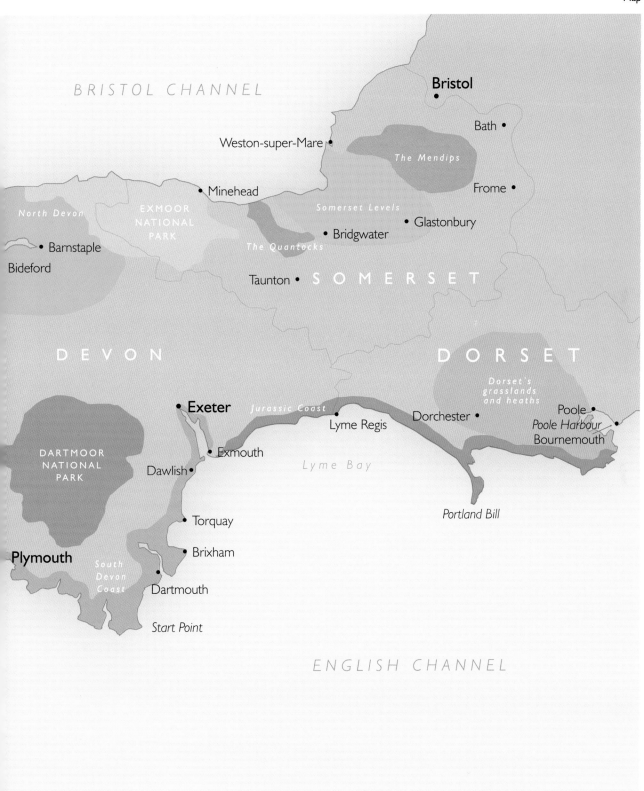

BRISTOL CHANNEL

Bristol •

Bath •

Weston-super-Mare •

The Mendips

Frome •

• Minehead

Somerset Levels

North Devon

EXMOOR
NATIONAL
PARK

• Glastonbury

• Bridgwater

• Barnstaple

The Quantocks

Bideford

Taunton • S O M E R S E T

D E V O N

D O R S E T

*Dorset's
grasslands
and heaths*

• **Exeter**

Jurassic Coast

Poole •

Dorchester •

DARTMOOR
NATIONAL
PARK

Lyme Regis

Poole Harbour
Bournemouth

• Exmouth

Lyme Bay

Dawlish •

*South
Devon
Coast*

Plymouth

• Torquay

Portland Bill

• Brixham

Dartmouth

Start Point

ENGLISH CHANNEL

1 Landscapes and Habitats
From submarine reef to moorland tor

From the lowest point on the coastal seabed to the highest moorland tor, the southwest of England has a hugely varied environment, providing a vast range of habitats for the region's plant and animal wildlife. That environment begins beneath the waves with rugged reefs, and extends through tidal mudflats, sandbars, beaches, dunes and saltmarshes, continuing on land with rivers, lakes and freshwater marshes, heaths, grasslands and woods, and finally the upland moors and bogs. Together, they all encapsulate the southwest's beautiful marine and terrestrial landscapes, along with the wildlife habitats they create.

Sea and coast

It is really no surprise that the sea figures large in the southwest's identity, hugely influencing the region's climate, environment and wildlife. Beneath the

Left: Spectacular sandstone rocks at Ladram Bay, at the western end of the Jurassic Coast World Heritage Site.

Above: A gnarled pine tree struggles to take hold in heathland on Winfrith Heath, near Wool, Dorset.

waves lies a world of dramatic contrasts that range from gentle sand, mud or shingle seabeds, to the wave-battered rocky pinnacles of a host of offshore reefs, coupled with the tidal rocks, sand and mud of the shoreline.

The intertidal zones of many of the rocky shores are well known for their rock pools, places where many marine plant and animal species can take refuge from the drying effects of the sun. Though popular as places to explore, far more famous are the southwest's spectacular sandy beaches. Scattered along the coast, long stretches of golden sand alternate with little intimate coves, many of them fronting onto either calmly lapping waters or furiously rolling surf, and backed by either rugged cliffs or soft rolling dunes.

Although the sandy beaches are generally not great wildlife habitats – at least not at low tide – accompanying dunes most definitely are. Generally stabilised by a range of grasses, many of the dunes' more sheltered parts are home to quite a surprising wealth of plants, including many beautiful, and often rare, wild flowers. For the most part, water drains rapidly through the dunes' sandy ground, so plants have to be tolerant of dry conditions. They must also be adapted to living in calcium-rich, rather alkaline soils, the result of

Above: Wind-whipped surf crashes over rocks at Widemouth Bay, Cornwall.

Left: A dusk view across rocks near Hartland Point, Devon.

Below: The southern end of the Penhale Dunes, at Perranporth, Cornwall.

Above: The most westerly of the Jurassic Coast's chalk cliffs, at Beer Head, with the older red sandstone cliffs in the distance.

the presence of millions of seashell fragments. However, some dunes do have pockets where water does not drain away well, resulting in 'dune slacks', sites of marshes or even open ponds, where aquatic plants can thrive.

Despite the large number of beaches, it is the cliffs that define much of the coastline. In the far west huge buttresses of granite stand defiantly against the Atlantic's rollers. Further east, these give way to gentler, more porous, often sedimentary rocks including, along Devon's south coast easily eroded red sandstone, and finally in Dorset limestone and gleaming white chalk.

These cliffs have created quite unique and very specialised habitats. What is able to live on them is highly dependent on such factors as the type of rock, how much (if any) soil cover there is, as well as typical rainfall, wind and salt spray exposures. Not surprisingly, moving from bare rock exposed to constant salt spray, to clifftops covered with at least a modicum of soil sees a rapid increase in the number of species. A softening of the climate also has an enormous influence. Dorset's relatively sheltered clifftops usually host rich grasslands that rapidly give way to farmland, for example, while north Cornwall's hugely exposed cliffs can generally manage only stretches of wind-stunted maritime heath and grasses.

Above: Chalk grassland in Fontmell Down Nature Reserve, near Shaftsbury, Dorset.

Conservation

Much of what we might think of as being wild or semi-wild landscapes exist as surviving remnants of a once much richer environment, today surrounded by towns and an intensively agricultural countryside. These surviving areas are increasingly coming into various forms of protection to save what is left, and to serve as biodiversity reservoirs from which it might eventually be possible to greatly improve the wider rural and coastal environments.

With such a rich, varied and beautiful countryside and coastline, it is not surprising that the southwest has a significant number of protected areas. These include of course two national parks (Exmoor and Dartmoor), two UNESCO World Heritage Sites (the Jurassic Coast and the Cornwall and West Devon Mining, the latter not relevant to this book), a UNESCO Biosphere Reserve (covering the north Devon coast and countryside), six

Above: Huge granite rocks make up the shoreline at Porthgwarra, a tiny fishing cove close to Land's End, Cornwall.

Ramsar sites (wetlands of major international importance for migratory birds, especially waterfowl), 38 National Nature Reserves (NNR), 10 Areas of Outstanding Natural Beauty (AONB), vast numbers of Sites of Special Scientific Interest (SSSI), and 20 Marine Conservation Zones (MCZ), the last of these the latest addition to the protected areas network. In addition, there are two types of EU protection, the Special Protection Area (SPA) and the Special Area of Conservation (SAC), the former aimed at protecting specific sites for specific bird species, the SACs intended to protect the most important sites for general wildlife conservation. The southwest has a large number of both such designations.

All this is in addition to the huge number of sites owned and protected by non-government organisations (NGOs), principally the National Trust and the six local groups of the Wildlife Trusts, but also including the Royal Society for the Protection of Birds (RSPB), and the Wildfowl and Wetlands Trust (WWT).

Altogether, it adds up to quite a wealth of bodies and protected areas aimed at safeguarding the future of the southwest's most precious landscapes, habitats and wildlife.

Above: A spring woodland view, the trees just leafing out, the ground covered with Bluebells, *Hyacinthoides non-scripta*, seen in Long Wood, Cheddar Gorge, Somerset.

25

Left: Curlews, *Numenius arquata,* feeding in shallow water over a mudflat in the estuary of the River Teign, Devon.

Bird life of the coasts and shores: Marine birds include of course the gulls, of which there are several species, including the herring gull (whose marauding behaviour gives all gulls a bad name), the black-headed gull, common gull, kittiwake, and the lesser and great black-backed gulls. Another common cliff bird that is frequently mistaken for a gull is the fulmar, which actually is a petrel, related to the albatrosses. The unmistakable terns consist here of mainly the common, little and sandwich species. Though they have breeding sites on Chesil Beach and in Poole Harbour, generally around the southwest they are seen only during the spring and autumn migrations.

Then there are the cormorants, shags and gannets. The last of these, spectacularly white with black-tipped wings, is sometimes seen hunting out to sea. Cormorants and shags, on the other hand, are a regular feature of harbours and rocky shores, their upright black bodies standing sentinel on a rock or swimming in the open water. Less easily seen are the puffins, guillemots and razorbills, which spend most of their life at sea, coming ashore for a few months only each year in order to breed.

Ducks, geese and waders are found largely in the calm shallow waters of estuaries, as well as inland marshes and lakes. There is quite a wide variety of waders, including herons, little egrets, curlews, redshanks, greenshanks, godwits, dunlins and plovers. The geese include Canada and Brent, while the most common of the many ducks include mallard, shelduck, shoveler, wigeon, teal, grebe and tufted duck. Swans are limited to the mute swan, the more northerly bewick's and whooper swans rarely coming this far south. The numbers of these birds swell vastly in winter, tens of thousands migrating in from northern breeding areas. One rare winter visitor is the beautiful avocet, in the southwest restricted largely to Poole Harbour and the estuaries of the Rivers Exe and Tamar.

Finally, two more birds of the water are the dipper and the iconic kingfisher, the latter hugely colourful and found on both still and moving water, the former a rather understated little brown and white bird that is restricted to fast-moving, rocky streams.

Above: Guillemots, *Uria aalge*, on the cliffs at Berry Head, Brixham, Devon.

Above: The much loved Puffin, *Fratercula arctica*, in the southwest is found only on Lundy and in the Isles of Scilly.

Above: A Sparrowhawk, *Accipiter nisus*.

Above: A Red Fox, *Vulpes vulpes*.

Bird life on land: On land the large range of habitats ensures an equally large diversity of bird types, varying from the tiniest wren, goldcrest and assorted tits up to the largest raptors, or birds of prey, that include the sparrowhawk, kestrel, peregrine falcon, buzzard and assorted owls, most especially the tawny and barn owls.

The raptors are the kings of the skies, buzzards frequently seen soaring high overhead, kestrels hovering over farmland or clifftops as they hunt for mice, a peregrine sometimes seen on a cliff or even church tower, occasionally glimpsed is it flashes past at high speed. The owls, being mostly nocturnal, are much harder to see, though tawny owls are frequently heard, the nights punctuated by their hoots and too-weets!

Many of our smaller birds are not at all easy to identify, particularly those in varying shades of brown. Nevertheless many garden and suburban birds are quite familiar, including the much-loved robin, the blackbird, thrush, starling, chaffinch, greenfinch, goldfinch, magpie, wood pigeon, the occasional nuthatch, the delightful blue and great tits, and of course the acrobatic swallows, swifts and martins, so much an integral part of summer.

Terrestrial mammals: The most well known of our mammals, of course, include the fox, badger, otter, grey squirrel, hedgehog, weasel, rabbit, hare and assorted deer, many of them spread right across the southwest's rural and suburban landscapes.

Above: Fallow Deer buck and doe, *Dama dama*, during the rutting season, in woodland near Launceston, Cornwall.

3 The Jurassic Coast
The southwest's World Heritage Site

Runnng from Orcombe Point, just east of Exmouth, in Devon, to Handfast Point, on the edge of Dorset's Studland Bay, a distance of 153 km (95 miles), is one of Europe's geologically most important stretches of coastline, the Jurassic Coast. For this reason it was awarded World Heritage Site status by UNESCO in 2001.

It is a spectacular succession of cliffs, rock arches, stacks and pebbly beaches that trace the Earth's geological evolution from the Triassic, through the Jurassic, to the Cretaceous Periods, a time line of about 250 to 65 million years ago. This is one of the best places in Britain to find fossils, many of the crumbling cliffs – particularly around Lyme Regis and Charmouth – yielding endless numbers, mostly tiny ammonites, but very occasionally even dinosaur parts.

Left: The cliffs at Burton Bradstock, just east of West Bay, on the Jurassic Coast of west Dorset.

Above: Old Harry Rocks, chalk cliffs and rocks at Handfast Point, the easternmost end of the Jurassic Coast World Heritage Site.

Above: Woodland in the Axmouth to Lyme Regis Undercliff, a national nature reserve on the Devon-Dorset border.

Certain areas of the coast are also important for wildlife conservation, particularly the small river estuaries in the easternmost part of Devon, the Undercliff just west of Lyme Regis, and the pebbly ramparts that make up the vast Chesil Beach, backed for much of its length by a brackish lagoon, the Fleet.

A journey through time

On moving eastwards from Exmouth, the Jurassic Coast's rocks evolve – with a few irregularities here and there – from Triassic orange-red sandstones in east Devon, through a Jurassic Period mixture of grey or yellow crumbly clay and solid limestones across much of Dorset, to brilliant white Cretaceous chalk in its eastern stretches, initially around Durdle Door and Lulworth Cove, and finally at its most spectacular at Handfast Point.

The 230 million-year-old Triassic red sandstone cliffs of east Devon were laid down at a time when this was a hot, dry desert, the rocks so coloured by the presence of large amounts of iron. Wildlife was scarce due to the harsh conditions, so fossils are few and far between.

By the time we reach Lyme Regis we are heading into clays and limestones of the Jurassic Period, a stretch of cliffs that are in a permanent state of collapse. Between Axmouth and Lyme, this has given rise to the Undercliff area, about 11 km (seven miles) long, site of an old cliff collapse that is now covered in dense semi-natural woodland, today a national nature reserve.

It is just to the east of Lyme Regis, however, particularly at Charmouth, where the cliffs are very fragile, attracting a constant stream of fossil collectors. These rocks were laid down at a time when the area was submerged under a shallow tropical sea that teemed with life. As a result, the area is a treasure trove of fossils, the most easily found embedded in limestone rocks along Monmouth Beach, just west of Lyme Regis. Here, hundreds of fossils can be seen, a handful really very large, the great majority just a few centimetres across. Almost all are ammonites, a now-extinct mollusc that lived in a spiral shell and which is closely related to today's squid, octopus and cuttlefish.

Thankfully, the fossils at Monmouth Beach are too well embedded to be taken away, so it is to Charmouth that fossil hunters generally head, the crumbling cliffs continually yielding up a fresh supply, at least for those prepared to take the risk of walking close to the fragile landslides. Again, most of the fossils are ammonites, along with many belemnites, a bullet- or pencil-shaped mollusc. However,

Above: A giant Ammonite fossil in rocks on the shore at Monmouth Beach, just west of Lyme Regis.

4 Dorset's Grasslands and Heaths

A land of flowers and insects

Left: A Bee Orchid, *Ophrys apifera*, an iconic orchid of Dorset's grasslands.

Above: Chalk grassland, with pink-flowering Pyramidal Orchids, *Anacamptis pyramidalis*, at Fontmell Down Nature Reserve, near Shaftsbury.

Dorset is well known for its open, rolling and grass-covered landscapes, with vistas that go on for miles across green hills, valleys and fields. It is a product of the largely chalky soil, very well drained, but mostly relatively infertile, ideal growing conditions for many of Britain's lime-loving, or calcareous, grasses and wild flowers. Streams and rivers are few and far between, most of the water percolating straight through the chalky soil to underground aquifers. The few waterways that do exist are mostly chalk streams, fed by the aquifers, a quite unusual environment, almost unique to a few counties of southern England.

This grassland landscape is spread across much of Dorset. In the southeast corner, however, things are quite different, for this is the home

Above: Ling Heather, *Calluna vulgaris*, and Dwarf Gorse, *Ulex minor*, in flower on heathland at Stoborough Heath National Nature Reserve, near Wareham.

Above: An Essex Skipper, *Thymelicus lineola*, a common butterfly of the grasslands.

of its heaths, lying mostly around the western and northern edges of Poole Harbour, with a few fragments further west, towards Dorchester. On the heaths, the land is generally rather low-lying and much less hilly than most of Dorset. The ground is mostly poorly drained, and over millennia peat has built up, generating the heathlands of today. The resulting largely acidic environment has created a quite different flora – and hence fauna too – from that on the chalky grasslands.

What these two distinct environments have in common is that they are quite endangered. It is thought that about 80% of both was lost during the 20th century, mostly to intensive agriculture – essentially ploughing and the widespread use of fertilizers and pesticides to improve the land's fertility. The chalky grasslands seem to be particularly sensitive to this, rapidly losing their biodiversity once ploughed and sprayed. Even land that in recent years has been taken out of intensive agriculture has been found to take a very long time to start to regain its wealth of native plant and animal species.

As a result, much of what remains is fragmented and not always in pristine condition. However, a large proportion of both the surviving chalky grasslands and heaths are now protected areas and are steadily being restored, creating a patchwork of increasingly beautiful and species-rich habitats right across the county.

The chalk grasslands

As already mentioned, chalk grasslands typify much of the rolling, hilly landscape of Dorset, even across landscapes that have largely been converted to intensive agriculture. It has to be admitted that, from a distance, at first glance and especially at certain times of the year, it can actually be not that easy to distinguish species-rich semi-natural grassland from a typical farm field. The distinction is further blurred by the fact that many of the protected grasslands are still used for agriculture, though almost exclusively traditional low impact methods of animal grazing and grass-cutting that have been used for hundreds of years.

The sensitivity of the chalk grasslands' biodiversity to modern farming methods has ensured that a large proportion of those that have survived to the present day are either old common lands or archaeological sites. A good many of Dorset's hills are crowned by the remains of prehistoric and Roman hill forts, today little more than grassy banks and ditches. While most of the old commons have only ever been subjected to low level traditional farming methods, in general the old hill forts have never seen a plough or agricultural chemicals. Good examples of such places include Powerstock Common, a beautiful mix of grassland, woodland and old railway cutting that is near Dorchester, and Hambledon Hill, a vast hill fort that is now a national nature reserve just north of Blandford Forum.

Above: A Six-spot Burnet, *Zygaena filipendulae*, on a Large Bird's-foot Trefoil flower, *Lotus pedunculatus*, in grassland in Kingcombe Meadows Nature Reserve, near Maiden Newton.

Below: The chalk grassland of Hambledon Hill, an ancient hill fort and national nature reserve.

Above: A mass of wild flowers in a meadow in Kingcombe Meadows Nature Reserve, near Maiden Newton.

In the summer months the semi-natural chalk grasslands really come into their own, a time when every patch of ground is a chaotic jumble of grasses, herbs, flowers and buzzing insects. Some estimates put the plant biodiversity alone as high as 40 species per square metre. Of course, while the professional conservationists will be as interested in the diversity of the grass species as anything else, for most people it is the plethora of stunning flowers that grab most attention. Perhaps most striking are the huge numbers of orchids, early purple orchids typical of spring, followed by spotted marsh orchids, pyramidal orchids and the stunningly lovely bee orchids, to name just four of the most well known.

Other flowers typical of the chalk grasslands include both bird's-foot and large bird's-foot trefoils, greater knapweed, yellow rattle, some cranesbills, field scabious, the ubiquitous ox-eye daisy and red clover. All these flowers attract a host of insects from grasshoppers to moths and butterflies, including the five- and six-spot burnet and mother shipton moths, silver-studded, meadow brown, ringlet, marbled white, the rare marsh fritillary and several species of skipper butterflies. The presence of water, such as around the chalk streams and occasional ponds, inevitably means dragonflies and damselflies, including the beautiful demoiselle, the azure damselfly and the scarce chaser.

The heaths

While the grasslands are a largely hilly landscape with alkaline soils, the heaths by contrast are mostly low-lying and acidic. Like the grasslands, Dorset's heaths have suffered badly at the hands of agriculture and urban development,

Above: A Large Bird's-foot Trefoil, *Lotus pedunculatus*, in Kingcombe Meadows Nature Reserve.

Above: A Cut-leaved Crane's-bill, *Geranium dissectum*, on Hambledon Hill, near Blandford Forum.

Above: Ling Heather, *Calluna vulgaris*, in Morden Bog, near Wareham.

Above: Common Self-heal, *Prunella vulgaris*, in Kingcombe Meadows Nature Reserve, near Maiden Newton.

Above: Common Spotted Orchid, *Dactylorhiza fuchsii*, in flower in Powerstock Common Nature Reserve, near Maiden Newton.

Above: Round-leaved Sundew, *Drosera rotundifolia*, on Winfrith Heath, near Wool.

Above: Greater Knapweed, *Centaurea scabiosa*, in Kingcombe Meadows Nature Reserve, near Maiden Newton.

Above: The very rare Marsh Gentian, *Gentiana pneumonanthe*, in Hartland Moor National Nature Reserve, near Wareham.

Below: Also rare, a Sand Lizard, *Lacerta agilis*, on gorse in Stoborough Heath National Nature Reserve, near Wareham.

the roughly 400 square kilometres (150 square miles) that existed 250 years ago now down to only about 80 square kilometres (30 square miles), much of what is left quite fragmented. These remaining areas are hugely important to conservation, representing about 10% of all the lowland heath in the UK, and 2% of that across Europe. Attempts are presently underway to reconnect some of the fragments into larger expanses of heathland in order to make them into viable and sustainable large-scale habitats.

Much of what remains – mostly now protected in a series of nature reserves – lies around the northern and western edges of Poole Harbour, particularly around the town of Wareham. Some parts of the heaths are quite dry, while others – principally the most low-lying areas – are very boggy even in mid-summer. Almost all areas are covered with heather and patches of gorse, as well as grasses. Most common in the drier areas are ling, bell heather and dwarf gorse, while the boggy regions are home to such plants as cross-leaved heath, bog asphodel and the carnivorous sundew. In a few of the wettest spots it is possible to find the very rare marsh gentian, a very beautiful violet-coloured flower. The dry areas are also home to Dorset heath, a heather species almost unique to Dorset's heathlands.

Animal wildlife includes quite a diversity of butterflies and dragonflies, but more importantly the heaths are home to all six of the UK's reptiles, namely the adder, smooth snake, grass snake, slow worm, common lizard and sand

lizard. The heathlands' most important bird species include the rather rare Dartford warbler, the nightjar (present only in summer) and the stonechat, the last of these very commonly seen perching on gorse bushes.

The coniferous woodlands that have grown over parts of Arne Nature Reserve are home to a large and very tame herd of sika deer, a species originally introduced from Japan. Arne is also notable for being on the western shore of Poole Harbour, a perfect location for observing the flocks of wading birds, including avocets and spoonbills, that make the harbour's shallows home, particularly in winter.

Apart from Arne, some of the most important heathland reserves include the contiguous Stoborough Heath and Hartland Moor, a short distance west of Arne. The boggy areas of Hartland are a good place to see the marsh gentian. To the north of Poole Harbour lies Holt Heath, the largest remaining area of heathland in Dorset, also site of some ancient woodland. To the west lies Morden Bog, a gently sloping heath, the upper, drier areas site of some of the area's oldest ling bushes, the lower parts Dorset's largest valley bog, home to bog myrtle, cotton grass and bog asphodel.

Perhaps the most well known of Dorset's heaths is Studland, a large tract of heather, gorse and scrub that contains a lake called the Little Sea, and which immediately adjoins not only Poole Harbour to the east, but also dunes and Studland Beach to the south.

Above: A Sika deer, *Cervus nippon*, in woodland in Arne Nature Reserve, near Wareham.

Places to visit

Powerstock Common and Kingcombe Meadows:

Two contiguous nature reserves owned by the Dorset Wildlife Trust, together covering about 300 hectares (740 acres) northwest of Dorchester. The reserves are a lovely mix of dry and wet/marshy grassland, semi-natural scrub and woodland, the course of an old railway line, a stream and riverside wet meadows.

Hambledon Hill:

Rising to a height of 192 metres (630 ft), the upper slopes of Hambledon Hill are covered by the grassy ramparts and ditches of an Iron Age hill fort, now a national nature reserve due to its huge plant diversity. Lying just north of Blandford Forum, the hill is quite a steep climb, but the reward is wonderful views and – in the summer months – a huge plethora of wild flowers and butterflies.

Fontmell Down:

A series of steep hillsides, this is a nature reserve managed by the Dorset Wildlife Trust, lying south of Shaftsbury. Covering 64 hectares (158 acres), this is one of Dorset's most species-rich grasslands, containing no less than nine species of orchid and 35 species of butterfly.

Arne:

A heathland nature reserve owned by the RSPB and lying on the western shore of Poole Harbour, Arne is a lovely mix of heather moor and conifer woods, with wonderful views across the harbour. Ling and bell heather are common, and in terms of birds this is an important place for the Dartford warbler, nightjar and stonechat. Birds of prey can often be seen, including merlin, marsh harrier and osprey. Huge numbers of wading birds can be seen on the harbour's mudflats, particularly in winter. A herd of sika deer adds extra interest, and are usually quite approachable.

Stoborough Heath and Hartland Moor:

Two contiguous national nature reserves to the south of Wareham, these consist of both dry and boggy heath, site of large amounts of the unique Dorset heath plant. The marshy areas also contain bog asphodel and marsh gentian. Common lizards, sand lizards and adders are frequently seen.

Studland Heath:

A national nature reserve owned by the National Trust, Studland immediately adjoins both Studland Beach and Poole Harbour. Easily accessible, it is probably the most heavily visited of the heaths.

Far left: A Yellowhammer, *Emberiza citrinella*, on Hambledon Hill, near Blandford Forum.

Left: A Meadow Brown butterfly, *Maniola jurtina*, on a Greater Knapweed, *Centaurea scabiosa*, in Kingcombe Meadows Nature Reserve, near Maiden Newton.

Below left: The orange fruiting bodies of Bog Asphodel, *Narthecium ossifragum*, surrounded by pink Cross-leaved Heath, *Erica tetralix*, in Hartland Moor National Nature Reserve, near Wareham.

Below right: A Scarce Chaser, *Libellula fulva*, a dragonfly, beside a pond in The Valley of Stones National Nature Reserve, near Portesham.

Bottom left: A Beautiful Demoiselle damselfly, *Calopteryx virgo*, in Kingcombe Meadows Nature Reserve, near Maiden Newton.

Bottom right: The lake known as the Little Sea, in Studland National Nature Reserve, near Poole.

5 The Mendip and Quantock Hills

Somerset's uplands

High hills, dense woodlands and open moorlands in Somerset? Must be Exmoor, surely. That would be most people's assumption, but they also belong to Somerset's two other hill ranges, the Mendips and Quantocks. Both relatively small in comparison to Exmoor, they are nevertheless hugely important features in the Somerset landscape, the Mendips stretching across much of the northern section of the county, separating Bristol from the rest of the southwest, the Quantocks sheltering the Taunton area from the Bristol Channel. Though neither has achieved national park status, both do have protection as Areas of Outstanding Natural Beauty (AONB).

Left: Bluebells and newly leafed-out woodland in early summer, in Long Wood, Cheddar Gorge.

Above: A lone, wind-sculpted conifer on heathland close to the summit of Wills Neck, highest point of the Quantock Hills.

Making comparisons

Both the Mendips and Quantocks rear up quite suddenly from the flat marshy lowlands of the Somerset Levels, the former at the Levels' northern limit, the latter just off their southwestern edge, and each is clearly visible from the other. And yet the two are surprisingly different, the Mendips underlain almost wholly by limestone, the Quantocks mostly by sandstone with some limestone areas.

The upshot is that the Mendips' quite rugged landscape is largely dry with few rivers running off them, instead rainwater both draining straight through the porous limestone into a honeycomb of caves and underground river systems, and eroding the landscape into a series of beautiful gorges. The Quantocks, by contrast, form a very solid-looking monolithic hill range running southeast to northwest, with a few small valleys along its edges but no gouged-out gorges and few caves below. What they do both have is ancient woodland nestling on some of the more sheltered slopes, the higher, more exposed areas given over to either rough moors or grassy pastures.

The Mendips: the lie of the land

The range of hills that usually falls under the name of the Mendips stretches roughly east-west, from almost as far east as Bath across to Brean Down on the Bristol Channel coast, just south of Weston-super-Mare. Their northern fringes reach almost the outskirts of Bristol, while the southern edge is clearly defined by a sharp escarpment rising above the Somerset Levels.

The AONB, however, takes in a rather smaller area, covering the Mendips' most rugged heartland, a roughly triangular shape of just under 200 square kilometres (77 square miles), ranging from just west of Shepton Mallet in the east and ending at Bleadon Hill, a little way short of Brean Down.

Above: The summit of Crook Peak, a prominent hill in the western part of the Mendips.

Right: A wind-gnarled Hawthorn tree, *Crataegus* species, on Brean Down, westernmost outrider of the Mendips.

6 The Somerset Levels
Restoring an ancient wetland landscape

The expanse of low-lying plains stretching across the heart of Somerset roughly from Wells and Weston-super-Mare in the north down to Taunton in the south, was once upon a time a vast watery landscape of marshes and low-lying islands. This was home to the Isle of Avalon, centred, so the stories go, on the historic town of Glastonbury.

Since then, of course an awful lot has changed. Many of the medieval villages can still be seen, sitting atop some of the little fingers of raised land – often barely worthy of the name 'hill' – that meander across the Somerset Levels and which were just high enough to keep the buildings above the marshes. The marshes, however, have largely gone, over the past 800 years drained to generate fertile agricultural land and to make accessible the valuable peat that formed the sodden base of the marshes.

Left: A showery spring day at the Catcott Complex Nature Reserves.

Above: A wintry view across marshes in Ham Wall National Nature Reserve, to Glastonbury Tor. Both reserves are part of the Avalon Marshes.

Naturally, the land remains very low-lying. Even as far inland as Glastonbury many of the fields are barely a metre above sea level, so winter flooding remains a constant threat, one that appears to be growing with rising sea levels and worsening winter storms, all very bad news for modern villages built on the flood plains, great news for the many thousands of migratory waterfowl that every winter call the Somerset Levels home.

Marshlands in today's Somerset Levels

Permanent wildlife-friendly marshes of any significant size are in general few and far between in today's Somerset Levels, though a number of ancient fragments do survive or have been restored from previous peat workings. All are now protected as important nature reserves, and collectively add up to a significant area, though still a minor percentage of the Levels' total land.

Prominent among these is a network of nature reserves a few miles west of Glastonbury, collectively known as the Avalon Marshes. Three of these reserves each cover about 100-200 hectares (250-500 acres), while the fourth takes up over 500 hectares (1240 acres). Since the reserves are close together, and in some places interlink, the total protected area comes to over 800 hectares (1980 acres), a not insignifcant area. The Avalon Marshes represent a major boost not just to wildlife conservation in the Levels but also to water management, helping to soak up some of the huge amounts of water that build up across the low-lying farmlands, particular during the winter.

Below: Marshy carr woodland in Shapwick Heath. Both Shapwick and Westhay are national nature reserves and part of the Avalon Marshes.

Right: The marshes of Westhay Moor, created by industrial-scale peat extraction, now a haven for wildlife.

but there should also be good numbers of teal, wigeon, shovelers, shelducks, lapwings, grebes and assorted geese, to name just the most obvious. Grey herons and little egrets should also put in fairly regular appearances, and increasingly the very rare (in the UK at least) great white egret. Relatively common in many parts of the warm temperate and tropical world, this bird seems to be slowly following in the footsteps of the little egret, which returned to this country after a long absence about 20 years ago. The even rarer European Spoonbill is also occasionally seen here.

Another heron that has recently returned to the Somerset Levels after a very long absence is the Eurasian bittern. Long extinct in the UK, the bittern returned to nature reserves on Britain's east coast a few years ago, but it is only since 2008 that it is known to have made the westward leap to the Somerset marshes. A shy little heron, it skulks secretively among the reeds, its brown markings providing almost perfect camouflage, particularly in winter. Although it is known to be living at least in the Westhay and Ham Wall reserves, sadly, the chances of seeing a bittern are not that great. However, in spring it will very likely be heard, its territorial call an utterly unique and quite bizarre booming noise.

Above: The ubiquitous Grey Heron, *Ardea cinerea*, is widespread just about anywhere that has water.

Below: By contrast, the *Eurasian Bittern*, *Botaurus stellaris*, is rare, spotted almost perfectly camouflaged among winter reeds in Ham Wall National Nature Reserve.

Places to visit

Westhay Moor National Nature Reserve:
Owned by the Somerset Wildlife Trust, Westhay is perhaps one of the southwest's most popular bird-watching sites. Its patchwork of lakes and carr woodland is criss-crossed by footpaths that lead to no less than six hides, two of them accessible to wheechairs.

Catcott Reserve:
Actually an aggregation of three smaller reserves, Catcott is also owned by the Somerset Wildlife Trust. A mix of marshy grassland, a small lake and an extensive area of carr woodland, this is one of the best places to catch a glimpse of roe deer and to see flocks of lapwing, as well as the usual ducks, herons and egrets. There are four hides scattered around the site, one of them next to the main car park.

Ham Wall National Nature Reserve:
Owned by the RSPB, Ham Wall consists of a vast network of reed-lined lakes and marshes, accessed largely by walking along the course of the long-defunct Highbridge-Glastonbury railway line. A good network of hides and screened viewpoints gives plenty of opportunity to view activity on the lakes. This is one of the best places in the southwest to see the elusive Eurasian bittern, as well as the rare marsh harrier.

Shapwick Heath National Nature Reserve:
At over 500 hectares (1240 acres), this is by some margin the largest of the Avalon Marshes reserves, and arguably the wildest. It consists largely of a mix of acidic grassland and carr woodland, the former site of a wide diversity of flowers in early summer. The main expanse of open water is Canada Lake, to the west of the main reserve, reached by a long woodland path that heads to a single rather remote hide.

Steart Marshes:
This vast new nature reserve has been created since 2012 jointly by the Environment Agency and the Wildfowl and Wetlands Trust. Consisting of a sprawling mass of newly formed tidal mudflats and saltmarshes in the estuary of the River Parrett, Steart is increasingly a winter home to thousands of migratory birds who move with the tides between these marshes and the mudflats of nearby Bridgwater Bay. Three beautiful new hides have been built next to a couple of the tidal lagoons.

Far left: A Great Crested Grebe, *Podiceps cristatus*, in winter plumage, on Canada Lake, Shapwick Heath National Nature Reserve.

Left: Marshy ground in Catcott Nature Reserve.

Below far left: Early spring in marshes in Westhay Moor National Nature Reserve.

Below left: Mute Swans, *Cygnus olor*, and a misty sunrise on the Sedgemoor marshes.

Below: Irises at dawn in the Sedgemoor marshes.

Bottom far left: A Mute Swan, *Cygnus olor,* in a wintry marsh landscape in Westhay Moor.

Bottom centre: *Phragmites* species reeds lit by wintry sunlight, in Ham Wall National Nature Reserve.

Bottom: A group of Wigeon, *Anas penelope*, in Catcott Nature Reserve.

77

7 Exmoor
Where the moors meet the sea

Welcome to a landscape of high rolling hills, a patchwork of farmland and open moors, dissected by deep, precipitous valleys that harbour dense, ancient woodlands, its northern borders crashing down via some of Britain's highest cliffs into the open sea. Exmoor is one of the most dramatic landscapes that anyone could hope to encounter in an otherwise gentle, homely southern England.

One of two national parks in southwest England, Exmoor straddles across both Somerset and Devon, though something like 70% lies within the former. This is the wild, remote, rugged Somerset, a total contrast to the flat low—lying Somerset Levels to the east.

Left: A mix of Bell Heather, *Erica cinerea*, and Western Gorse, *Ulex gallii*, in flower on Bossington Hill, with a view across Porlock and along the Bristol Channel coast.

Above: A view of woodlands, farmland and moors, a typical scene in Exmoor National Park, seen from County Gate, near Lynmouth.

Hills and moors

Covering an area of 692 square kilometres (267 square miles), much of Exmoor is not moor at all but farmland, particularly along its southern, inland slopes, over the centuries the wild and often boggy moorlands slowly drained and improved for agriculture, a process that only came to an end in the latter part of the 20th century.

The fact that it has survived at all in a still relatively wild state is down to the protection it received for many hundreds of years – beginning in Norman times and ending in the Victorian period – as a royal hunting forest. That protection thankfully resumed in 1954 when Exmoor was declared a national park.

Today, about a quarter of the national park remains open moorland, mostly as a central 'belt' across the tops of the highest, remotest hills, places where the harsh weather blowing in off the sea makes life tough even for heather, gorse and bilberry. This is a landscape where the hills draw majestically sweeping skylines, the rounded outlines dropping from the summits in graceful arcs that somehow transform into steep, plunging descents down into narrow, shadowy valleys that cut like a series of knives between the hills.

Below: A moorland Hawthorn tree, *Crataegus* species, silhouetted against a dusk sky, near Simonsbath.

Above: An evening view of the edge of Horner Wood, where it meets the moors of Dunkery Beacon.

Even the park's north-facing coastline is like this, many of Exmoor's highest coastal hills ending quite precipitously, some of those plunging descents suddenly turning into dramatic vertical cliffs as if the land had been chopped with an axe. The highest cliffs in England can be found here, those below the ominously named Great Hangman dropping 244 metres (800 ft) to the sea.

Inland, king of the hills is Dunkery Beacon, at 519 metres (1703 ft) Exmoor's highest peak, a vast rolling behemoth of a hill, its upper slopes open moorland, its lower southern and northwestern flanks enclosed grazing farmland. Its moorland areas are, frankly, rather bleak and featureless for much of the year, though it is transformed to a place of great beauty during the July-September heather flowering period. To the north, Dunkery plunges down into a deep valley that houses Horner Woods, a large area of semi-natural ancient oak woodlands. All this area – Horner Woods and the Dunkery massif – are triply protected for their nature conservation importance, not only enclosed within the national park but also owned by the National Trust and designated a national nature reserve (one of three on Exmoor).

Above: Ling Heather, *Calluna vulgaris*, in flower on the summit of Dunkery Beacon, Exmoor's highest point.

Above: Storridge Woods seen in early autumn in the south of Exmoor, near Wimbleball Lake.

Exmoor woodlands

Horner is perhaps the largest of Exmoor's valley ancient woodlands, though there are many others. Both of the moor's two other national nature reserves are such woodlands, Hawkcombe Woods just to the northwest of Horner, and Tarr Steps Woodland, a rather long, narrow woodland lining the banks of the River Barle on the southern edge of the national park. Its name is taken from the prehistoric bridge that crosses the River Barle in the midst of these woodlands.

Other valley woodlands include the beautiful and much visited Watersmeet, owned by the National Trust and lining the East Lyn River, along a very deep narrow valley just to the south of Lynmouth. Along the southern edges of the park are Storridge Wood, close to Wimbleball Lake (a large modern reservoir) and a collection of woodlands around the town of Dulverton, the national park's southern gateway. All these woods are predominantly oak, though ash, hazel, holly and birch are also common, with hawthorn and rowan common along the woodland-moorland fringes. They also harbour several rare species of whitebeam tree, some found nowhere else.

Rather unique to Exmoor is the coastal woodland that runs along parts of the most inaccessible stretches of coastline, mainly to the west of Porlock.

Below: The lovely waterfall at Watersmeet, near Lynmouth.

Much of this is also oak, though often rather stunted and gnarled by the harsh coastal weather. That they can grow here at all is quite remarkable, and is probably down to their northeast orientation, the high hills behind giving some protection from the worst of the maritime weather.

The rivers

The bogs that characterise much of Exmoor's open moorland form the headwaters for a number of rivers that drain down through the valleys towards the lowlands. Despite its position on the north coast, most of these rivers merge to create the River Exe, which flows southwards, cutting right across Devon to reach the sea on the south coast just south of Exeter. The River Barle is perhaps the largest of the tributaries that merges with the Exe, though the Exe itself has its source on moorland northwest of the village of Simonsbath.

A few rivers do make short steep, foaming descents from the hills northwards to the north coast, perhaps the most well known of these the East and West Lyn Rivers, which merge and reach the sea at Lynmouth.

A wildlife haven

Exmoor is a rich environment for much of southern England's wildlife, said to be home to almost 250 species of bird, over 1000 species of plant, and many of the mammals that typify the English countryside. These of course include the usual badgers, rabbits and foxes, but also weasels (which seem to be particularly bold here), hares, and otters. As with other areas of the southwest, Exmoor remained something of a stronghold for the otter during times when it was almost wiped out across most of England, and today it can be found in all of the national park's rivers.

However, there is one mammal which is quite iconic for Exmoor: the red deer. Exmoor is home to the southwest's principal red deer herd, consisting of over 3000 animals. Although notoriously shy, they are not always that difficult to find, once you know where to look, and during the autumn rutting season Exmoor has become the place *par excellence* to come to watch.

Above: The upper reaches of the River Barle, near Simonsbath, seen in evening sunlight.

Above: The Weasel, *Mustela nivalis*, is common across Exmoor's countryside.

Above: A large Red Deer stag guards his harem during the rutting season, on open moorland near Exford.

Above: The lovely Dipper, *Cinclus cinclus*, is common on Exmoor's fast-flowing streams, seen here at Watersmeet, near Lynmouth.

Right: A Red Deer hind (or female), *Cervus elaphus*, with a its foal, seen near Dunster.

Throughout much of the year red deer can be seen at dawn on the moorland parts of Dunkery Beacon, for example, though during the daytime they usually retreat to the woodlands or scrub to hide. Even if on the open moor they can be amazingly difficult to spot: although the heather, gorse and bracken do not grow all that high and red deer are really rather large, as soon as they sit down they completely merge with the vegetation.

Although red deer steal the limelight, Exmoor's woodlands are also home to a good many fallow and roe deer, both significantly smaller than the reds (particularlly the roe deer), and because they spend most of their time in woodlands much harder to spot.

In terms of birds, both woodland and moorland species are common. Out on the moors, meadow pipits, wheatears and stonechats are commonly found, the last of these frequently seen perching prominently on gorse bushes, while overhead cruise a number of birds of prey, most especially the ubiquitous buzzard and kestrel.

Down on the rivers, pied and grey wagtails are commonly seen flitting from one waterside rock to another, while the truly iconic bird of this habitat is the dipper. A remarkable little bird that has become the emblem of the Devon Wildlife Trust, the dipper is rather robin-like in appearance, but coloured brown, chestnut and white. It spends its time hopping from one mid-stream rock to another, dipping its head under water to catch crustaceans and insects, and even frequently diving in to swim with the current.

8 North Devon Landscapes and Seascapes
A Biosphere Reserve

From the Exmoor border at Combe Martin westwards to the Cornish border at Marsland, the north Devon coast is a succession of rocky cliffs, sandy beaches and dunes, broken only by the lovely estuary of the Taw and Torridge Rivers, the two rivers that drain north Devon. Inland, the countryside is generally agricultural, but there are also fragments of a once much more common environment, the culm grasslands. While not immediately beautiful, close-up in summer the culm areas do have an intense beauty, the rough, tussocky grasslands carpeted with an array of wild flowers, alive with a host of buzzing and fluttering insects.

Left: The fantastic rock formations for which Morte Point is renowned, near Mortehoe.

Above: The sand dunes of Woolacombe Beach.

Above: Rocks, pools and the vast expanses of sand at Saunton Sands, near Barnstaple.

The entire coastline above the waves is protected within the North Devon Coast Areas of Outstanding Natural Beauty, while large chunks of what lies below the waves have been declared Marine Conservation Zones (MCZs), including the waters around the island of Lundy. Inland, most of what survives of the culm grassland is now protected as a network of nature reserves, while much of the wider countryside is included in the North Devon Nature Improvement Area, a scheme intended to help farmers and local residents improve the wildlife value of the countryside.

On top of all this, UNESCO has declared the region a Biosphere Reserve, covering 3300 square kilometres (1274 square miles) of countryside, coast and sea, its core centred on the internationally important Braunton Burrows sand dune complex.

The culm grasslands

Rough, tussocky, unimproved grassland formed over acidic, poorly drained clay soils, and which down the centuries has only been used for grazing, over the past 100 years over 90% of the culm grassland has been lost, with nearly half going between 1984 and 1991, largely under the plough and the fertilizer spray, but also to overgrazing and encroachment of scrub and woodland.

Above: The lovely diminutive Water Forget-me-Not, *Myosotis scorpioides*, in marshy culm grassland at Meresfelle Nature Reserve, near Bideford.

In the early 2000s conservation groups started to rescue the surviving fragments, protecting not just healthy culm, but also some that had undergone agricultural improvement in the past, and which are now being helped to revert to culm grassland.

Although culm grassland is not a particularly beautiful landscape, the profusion of wild flowers and insects during the summer months makes it all worthwhile. Only plants that like wet, acidic, poorly fertilized conditions will thrive here, but fortunately quite a few fit that requirement. Several orchids are particularly common, especially the heath spotted and southern marsh orchids, along with such flowers at St John's wort, ragged robin, meadowsweet and wild angelica. Really boggy parts frequently contain such beauties as bog asphodel, bog bean, water forget-me-not, cotton grass and sundew.

Above: Barn Owls, *Tyto alba*, are relatively common across the culm grasslands.

Above: Perforate St John's Wort, *Hypericum perforatum*, seen in the culm grasslands of Knowstone Moor.

Left: The beautiful yellow flowers of Bog Asphodel, *Narthecium ossifragum*, a rare plant, though commonly seen in the marshy areas of Devon's culm grasslands. Seen here at Knowstone Moor Nature Reserve.

Above: The tiny Sand Pansy, *Viola tricolor ssp curtisii*, found at a handful of coastal sites around the UK, seen here in the dunes of Braunton Burrows.

Butterflies and moths are common, including the endangered marsh fritillary, while bird life includes barn owls, snipe, curlews, reed buntings, willow tits, and grasshopper warblers. Mammals include the harvest mouse, fox, otter and several species of bat. The presence of scrub and woodland allows the presence of roe deer, and some reserves also have red deer.

Along the coast: estuary and dunes

The coast ranges from high cliffs to sandy beaches and dunes, all split in two by the waters of the Taw-Torridge estuary, whose mudflats are one of numerous coastal sites in the southwest important to the feeding and refueling of migratory waterfowl.

Fringing the northern edge of this estuary is this coast's single most important habitat, the enormous Braunton Burrows sand dunes, covering an area 5 x 1.5 km (3 x 1 miles), one of the three largest dune complexes on the UK's west coast. To seaward stretches the vast Saunton Sands beach, the dunes rearing up immediately behind in several waves, the highest up to 30 metres (98 ft). About 400 species of plant have been found in these dunes, from the grasses such as marram and dune fescue, to such beautiful flowers as southern marsh orchid, pyramidal orchid, viper's bugloss, bitter stonecrop, mellilot, greater yellow rattle and evening primrose. One of the rarer flowers is the tiny and delicately beautiful sand pansy, found only at a scattering of sites around the British coast.

Above: A snippet of the vast range of dunes that make up Braunton Burrows National Nature Reserve.

Along the coast: rocks and cliffs

To the north of Braunton Burrows, the coast is a mix of rocky headlands and sandy beaches, the latter most famously consisting of Croyde Bay and the huge Woolacombe Sands. For rocks and headlands there are Baggy, Morte and Bull Points, plus Rockham Bay, all rugged places with interesting rock formations and many of the usual coastal flowers, such as thrift and sea campion. Grey seals can frequently be seen in rocky inlets on remoter parts of this coast.

West of the Taw-Torridge estuary the coast is steep but quite sheltered. On either side of the village of Clovelly is another stretch of coastal woodland similar to those found along Exmoor's coast. As on Exmoor these woodlands are quite difficult to access and are largely undisturbed. Their steep slopes also face northeast, again ensuring good protection from the maritime southwest winds.

Things change dramatically at Hartland Point. Not only is this headland itself quite rugged, but here the coast turns abruptly southwards, becoming exposed to the full force of the Atlantic's winds. From here to the Cornish border is Devon's wildest and remotest coastline. The cliffs are high and sheer, the rocks sliced and jagged; here and there waterfalls cascade down the cliffs straight onto the shore. In places, successive layers of sedimentary orange sandstones and mudstones have been forced into insane angles,

Above: The wonderful waterfall at Speke's Mill Mouth, near Hartland Quay.

Above: The spectacular Hartland coastline just south of Hartland Point.

twisted into all kinds of swirling curves, diagonals and even chevrons. The patterns are the result of huge tectonic forces about 300 million years ago, when two continental plates collided, at one side of what is now Europe creating the Alps, to the west resulting in these astonishing cliff patterns.

Lundy

Lying 19 km (12 miles) off the north Devon coast, Lundy is a long, narrow north-south island, about 5 km (three miles) long, guarding the entrance to the Bristol Channel, and consisting mainly of a high, gently rolling, almost treeless plateau ringed by enormous, windswept cliffs.

Below: The cliffs of the west coast of Lundy Island are as rugged as any found throughout the southwest of England.

Its name is the Icelandic word for puffin, suggesting both historic Nordic connections and importance to wildlife. Today, puffins are much less common on Lundy than they once were, though successful eradication of rats from the island is now helping their recovery. The cliffs and rocks are, however, home to large numbers of other birds, including fulmars, cormorants, guillemots, razorbills and kittiwakes, as well as some puffins, and gannets are regularly seen offshore. Grey seals are common, and at low tide it is possible to get quite close to them in a cove next to the ferry jetty. Dolphins are also regularly spotted around the island and basking sharks are occasional visitors.

Above: A Grey Seal, *Halichoerus grypus*, perches on a rock just off the southwest shore of Lundy Island.

9 Dartmoor

Devon's wild heart

D artmoor National Park, at the very heart of Devon, has some of the
remotest and most rugged landscapes in southwest England. From
desolate, open moorland on the high hills, to dense and ancient oak
woodlands in the deep, narrow valleys, this is one of Britain's most beautiful
rural environments.

At 954 square kilometres (368 square miles), the park is among the
largest protected landscapes in the southwest. Locally, its rolling hills are
generally divided into the high moor and the low moor, the latter consisting
mainly of farmland, forest and scattered villages, the high moors the wide
open, largely treeless landscapes where sheep, ponies and cattle are more or
less free to roam at will.

Left: The River Tavy flowing through
moorlands in the Tavy Cleave.

Above: The iconic Brent Tor, on the
western edge of Dartmoor National Park,
and near Tavistock.

The high moor

It is this open moorland that constitutes the quintessential Dartmoor landscape. Though mostly desolate and windswept, its wide vistas and open spaces are quite literally a breath of fresh air in an otherwise crowded southern England. To some, the high moor's space, emptiness and almost constant wind are invigorating and liberating, while to others it is just bleak, wet and depressing. It can of course be all those, sometimes changing from one to the other in minutes.

The landscape is not dramatic in the way that the mountains of Scotland are, though it certainly is rugged. The hills roll in a series of waves, here and there diving down into some deep narrow valley. Many of the hills are topped by a tor, a pinnacle of granite, sometimes completely solid, often a jumble of boulders, that are an absolutely defining feature of Dartmoor's high moorland landscape.

Below: The granite boulders of Bonehill Rocks, with a view across open moors, seen on a stormy winter's day, near Widecombe-in-the-Moor.

Heather, gorse, bracken and grasses cover much of this landscape, and a considerable proportion of it can be very wet indeed, much of it consisting of blanket bogs, permanent marshlands. These are the sources of most of Devon's rivers, including the Dart, Teign, Avon, Yealm, Erme, Plym, Tavy and Torridge, all of which start as swamps and bogs on the high moor. Dartmoor's largely granite base prevents most of the water from filtering downwards through the ground, ensuring that it sits at or close to the surface in marshes, before flowing downhill in a myriad of streams and rivers.

Above: Saddle Tor, with Haytor in the distance, on a calm snow-covered winter's day. Dartmoor gets some of the southwest's worst winter weather.

The low moor

The low moor, by contrast, has a much more homely feel, characterised largely by steep narrow valleys, mostly along Dartmoor's largely sheltered eastern and southern flanks, though also sometimes in little pockets surrounded by the high moor. It's in the low moor areas that you'll find the majority of Dartmoor's villages, clusters of weather-beaten granite cottages, surrounded by farms and farmland, the fields usually tiny and enclosed within massive granite walls, overgrown with the thorny likes of brambles, hawthorn and blackthorn.

Above: A wind-gnarled Hawthorn, *Crataegus* species, silhouetted against a low winter sun.

It is also here that most of Dartmoor's woodlands grow, hunkering down in the valleys, away from the often severe weather sweeping the high moors. These valleys have been gouged out by Devon's rivers, draining the moorland swamps above, splashing and gurgling their way downhill towards the sea, usually along some very picturesque granite boulder-strewn watercourses, overhung by dense stands of oak and beech forest. These woodlands are Dartmoor's verdant gem, moss-draped old oaks leaning out across the flowing waters, in autumn the beech trees throwing out a splash of gold as a final display before winter sets in.

A wildlife refuge: the plants

Firstly, there are of course the woodlands themselves, consisting largely of oak and beech trees, frequently with a colonising band of silver birch around the outer edges, where woodland meets open moor. Down in the sheltered valleys, particularly along the river banks, the trees can reach quite considerable sizes, shrinking to stunted and gnarled forms higher up the valley sides, where the soil is thinner and there is greater exposure to the moorland weather.

The most extensive and well-known of these woodlands spread along the valleys of the Rivers Teign, Bovey, Dart, Plym and Tavy. They are so important to nature conservation that many are protected not just within the national park but still further within either national nature reserves (as with the woodlands of the Dart Valley) or in National Trust ownership (as with some of the Teign valley woodlands).

The open moor is mostly devoid of trees, apart from a scattering of hardy, wind-blasted hawthorns and rowans. However, a few pockets of truly ancient woodland do survive here. The last surviving fragments of what is

Above: A view of the upper Dart Valley and the ancient oak woodlands that make this a national nature reserve.

Right: A rainbow arches across marshy moorland and a lone Hawthorn, *Crataegus* species, on Gidleigh Common, near Chagford.

Far right: The River Dart flowing through the ancient oak woodlands, *Quercus* species, of the Dart Valley National Nature Reserve, downstream of Dartmeet.

Above: Common Snowdrops, *Galanthus nivalis*, are one of Dartmoor's earliest harbingers of spring.

Below: The gnarled and moss-covered Oaks, *Quercus petraea*, of Wistman's Wood National Nature Reserve, constitute one of the few remaining fragments of genuinely ancient woodland left on the high moor.

probably natural forest that once cloaked the high moor, these tiny, fragile woodlands are quite different from most of their valley cousins. Characterised by stunted and gnarled oak trees, their twisted branches are covered and hung with layers of soggy moss and ferns, the ground frequently boulder-strewn, but largely hidden by moss and bilberry bushes. Most well known of these little woodlands is Wistman's Wood, protected as a national nature reserve, and hidden away in the heart of the high moor near the Two Bridges hamlet.

Most of the woodlands protect a wealth of wild flowers, many of which struggle to grow beyond the tree cover. These include the wood anemone, frequently seen in Dartmoor's woodlands, its clusters of white flowers one of the earliest harbingers of spring. The incredible slowness with which it is able to colonise new ground makes it an invaluable indicator of a truly ancient woodland – if its flowers and leaves carpet a woodland floor then that woodland must have been there a very long time!

Other flowers typical of Dartmoor's woodlands and hedgerows include the snowdrop and the ubiquitous three-cornered leek, both quite early flowering. Coming rather later is the surprisingly delicate wild garlic (also called the ramson), often flowering simultaneously and alongside the universally loved bluebell. Spring has well and truly arrived when the bluebell comes into flower, carpeting not just some of Dartmoor's woodlands but also some areas of treeless open moorland. Few experiences are more quintessentially Dartmoor than to stand among a sea of bluebells on open moorland, with the sound of a cuckoo calling in the distance.

Above: The true Wild Daffodil, *Narcissus pseudonarcissus*, the wild antecedent of all the garden varieties, is quite rare, but can be found in several Dartmoor woods, such as at Dunsford.

Top far left: The rocky cliffs of Dodman Point.

Top middle: A Speckled Wood butterfly, *Pararge aegeria*, in woodland on Dodman Point.

Top right: Autumnal oak woodland on a misty morning along the West Looe River.

Far left middle: Early morning sunlight in Portnadler Bay, near Looe.

Far left bottom: Sunrise over Looe Island.

Left: On a stormy day surf thunders onto rocks at Perprean Cove, near Coverack.

Above: Rock Samphire in flower, *Crithmum maritimum*, at Portnadler Bay.

12 North Cornwall Coast and Moors

The rugged Atlantic landscape

Exposed to the full force of the Atlantic, this is the wild heart of Cornwall, the coastline a place of high rocky cliffs interspersed with long sandy beaches and dunes, the inland areas a patchwork of small farms and largely treeless moors and heaths. Here and there a few small woodlands survive, but only in those valleys that are sheltered from the Atlantic winds.

The moors range from the high hills of Bodmin Moor to lowland fragments, generally consisting of poorly drained acidic soils that have created heather- and gorse-covered heathlands, as well as marshes, bogs and ponds.

Left: Marram Grass, *Ammophila arenaria*, on the Holywell dunes, with a view across the beach to Penhale Point and Carter's Rocks.

Above: With an Atlantic storm approaching, surf pounds the beach at Widemouth Bay.

Above: Surf crashes around the cliffs of The Mouls, an island off Rumps Point, near Polzeath.

Below: Early morning sunlight on Lye Rock, seen from Bossiney, near Boscastle.

The coast is a seemingly endless series of spectacular cliffs, headlands, coves and bays. This is the land of the long white beach, iconic stretches of sand that are the hallmark of Cornwall. Some of them are backed by dunes whose grasslands are vital to conservation, while the cliftops are covered largely by maritime heath.

As with Cornwall's south coast, much of the region is protected, often with multiple designations, ranging from National Trust and Cornwall Wildlife Trust ownership and enclosure within the Cornwall AONB, to SSSI and nature reserve status, as well as several SACs and newly designated MCZs.

Bodmin Moor

Cornwall's only upland massif, Bodmin Moor is underlain by granite and site of extensive heaths, marshes and bogs, all topped by a series of granite tors. It is in this environment that the Camel, Fowey and Lynher Rivers all rise. The Moor's highest points are Brown Willy (420 m/1378 ft) and Rough Tor (400 m/1312 ft), surrounded by a treeless landscape, a mix of grassland, wet heathland and blanket bogs. North of Rough Tor is Crowdy Marsh, an important wetland breeding site for such birds as snipe, curlew, black-headed gull and lapwing. Birdlife International has declared Bodmin Moor an Important Bird Area due to the large numbers of breeding stonechats and over-wintering golden plovers.

Some of Cornwall's best woodlands lie in Bodmin Moor's southern valleys, most especially at Golitha Falls in the valley of the River Fowey. A beautiful series of stepped waterfalls, Golitha and its surrounding woodlands are a national nature reserve, the steep valley sides cloaked in ancient oak trees. The reserve is important for mosses and liverworts, 120 species recorded here, while dormice and several species of bat – noctule, brown long-eared and lesser horseshoe – also live here. Otters, as well as salmon and sea trout, are known to use the river.

Above: Autumnal sunlight on the open moors of Rough Tor, one of the highest points of Bodmin Moor.

Above: Ancient woodland crowds in around the River Fowey at Golitha Falls, a national nature reserve.

Above: The flowers of Dorset Heath, *Erica ciliaris.*

Above: The delicate pink flowers of Common Centaury, *Centaurium erythraea.*

Below: Marsland Wood, sheltered in a deep, narrow valley.

Lowland moors

A rather similar heathland environment to Bodmin Moor, the lowland moors survive as small scattered fragments. At 480 ha (1186 acres) Goss Moor is by far the largest survivor, protected as both an SSSI and a national nature reserve. It is also part of an SAC, in combination with nearby Breney Common and Tregoss Moor. Some of the wettest parts of Goss Moor form the headwaters of the River Fal. The heaths are rich in heathers and western gorse, while Carrine Common is one of only a handful of UK sites outside Dorset to have the rare Dorset heath.

Goss Moor is protected for its many rare species, including such plants as yellow centaury, two species of St John's wort and marsh cinquefoil, as well as the marsh fritillary butterfly and the European nightjar. Overall, Goss Moor is home to 29 species of butterfly, 18 dragonflies and damselflies, and 70 species of breeding birds.

Coastal woodlands

With the massive exposure that Cornwall's north coast has to the Atlantic winds, it seems remarkable that there are any woodlands at all here. However, there is a scattering of generally very small woods, most of them nestling in well sheltered, almost hidden, valleys.

Perhaps the most well known is Marsland Wood, running along the sides of a narrow valley that straddles the Devon-Cornwall border within a couple of miles of the coast. Mostly dense oak woodland near the valley floor, the trees become increasingly stunted as the valley approaches the coast, and

disappear altogether within a few hundred metres of the shore, replaced by grassland, patches of scrub and stands of foxgloves. Within the woods there are occasional flower-rich wet meadows.

Further south is another similar valley woodland, the National Trust-owned Coombe Valley, while further south again, just south of Widemouth Bay, is the Woodland Trust-owned Millook Valley Woods. Just west of here, on the cliffs at Dizzard Point, is arguably Cornwall's most remarkable woodland: clifftop wind-stunted oak trees, largely exposed to the Atlantic winds, but managing to survive nonetheless.

Sand dunes

Most of the sandy beaches are backed by rocky cliffs, but a number are lined by sand dunes, usually stabilised by a range of sand- and calcium-loving grasses and flowers (the calcium coming from millions of seashell fragments). The main

Above: A Common Foxglove, *Digitalis purpurea*, at Marsland Mouth.

dune sites occur at Constantine Bay just west of Padstow, at Rock inside the Camel estuary, and at Holywell Bay just southwest of Newquay. However, by far the largest are the Penhale Dunes, running northwards for several miles from the vast beach at Perranporth, making Penhale one of the largest dune areas in southwest England.

The Penhale and Holywell Dunes almost meet, and together have been designated a single SAC for their wide plant biodiversity. Relatively common plants include common centaury, kidney vetch, pyramidal orchid, meadowsweet, water mint and great willowherb. Some rarer plants include Babington's leek, shore dock, sea spurge, and early gentian.

The rugged cliffs

The magnificent cliff views take the limelight along this coast. A complex geology and constant battering from

Right: The dunes at Holywell Bay.

Above: Surf crashes against the rocks and cliffs of Bedruthan Steps, north of Newquay.

the harsh Atlantic weather ensure a jagged wildness to both the cliff faces and the jumble of offshore rocks, that sets the mood for this fantastic landscape.

One of the most famous of all Cornish views is that of Bedruthan Steps, a line of huge surf-battered islets standing a short distance off the main cliffs. Lying between Newquay and Padstow, it is an iconic view that encapsulates the ruggedness of this coast, the huge dark rocks standing solidly and stoically against the swirling white surf.

Apart from this, there are uncountable numbers of stunning views all along the coast. These include the incredible striations and swirls of uplifted and twisted sedimentary rocks at Sandy Mouth near Bude (similar to those in the Hartland cliffs of Devon; pages 93-94), the lines of rocks that enclose the southern end of Widemouth Bay, the imposing cliffs at Bossiney, and the rugged twin headlands of Rumps Point and Pentire Point, to name just a few personal favourites.

Most of the cliffs are topped by gorse- and heather-covered heaths, the former largely low-growing western gorse, the heather consisting mainly of ling and bell heather, with cross-leaved heath in the wetter areas. A few patches of Dorset heath can be found, particularly around St Agnes Head.

Maritime flowers are of course very common, including thrift and sea campion, and here and there 'meadows' of clifftop flowers can be seen, including a large expanse of bluebells on the cliffs above Boscastle harbour, and a huge variety of flower types on Pentire Point West near Newquay.

Above: A yellow-flowering Kidney Vetch, *Anthyllis vulneraria*, a common clifftop flower.

Above: Bluebells, *Hyacinthoides non-scripta*, spread across the clifftops above Boscastle harbour.

Top: Fulmars, *Fulmarus glacialis*, are common marine birds, nesting on the cliffs of the Cornish coast.

Above: A Shag, *Phalacrocorax aristotelis*, seen at Duckpool, near Bude.

Above and below these clifftops seabirds constantly circle, herring and great black-backed gulls, cormorants, shags and fulmars all frequently seen and heard, while gannets can sometimes be seen patrolling offshore. Dolphins and grey seals are also regular sights, the latter particularly in the remoter coves around some of the headlands, the former usually further out.

Beneath the waves, this coast is renowned for its rocky reefs. Wildlife is typical of such a rugged habitat, with kelp seaweeds clinging to the rocks in shallower waters, sponges, anemones and pink sea fan corals in deeper areas. North of Tintagel these submarine habitats form the southern extension of the Hartland Point to Tintagel MCZ, while the adjacent cliffs and land are protected as an SAC.

Sheltered waters

Shelter is scarce. Unlike Cornwall's south coast, there are few river estuaries, the only really significant one that of the Camel River. As with the south coast estuaries, the river itself is comparatively small, most of its valley actually a tidal marine environment, covered with sea water at high tide, a vast expanse of mudflats and sandbars at low tide. The higher reaches, towards Wadebridge, contain mudflats and marshes that are important to wading birds.

At the river's mouth the Camel joins the sea in a large bay, sheltered to the northeast by the rugged Pentire Point and to the west by Stepper Point. All of this bay, plus coastal waters stretching for several miles west and east, has recently come under protection as an MCZ, protecting very similar habitats and species to those described for the Hartland Point to Tintagel MCZ, as well as intertidal sands in the Camel estuary.

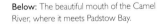

Below: The beautiful mouth of the Camel River, where it meets Padstow Bay.

Places to visit

Rough Tor:
One of the highest points on Bodmin Moor, a granite boulder-topped tor with stunning views and an expanse of moorland grass and heath. Reachable by car from Camelford as far as a car park at the foot of the tor, followed by a steep 20 minute hike to the summit.

Golitha Falls:
A beautiful waterfall, a stepped series of cascades, on the River Fowey, set in dense oak woodland in a sheltered valley on the southern edge of Bodmin Moor. Lots of bluebells and wood anemones here in spring.

Marsland Wood:
A rare woodland on Cornwall's north coast, straddling the border with Devon. The trees are sheltered from the Atlantic winds in a steep, narrow valley.

Rumps and Pentire Points:
Twin rugged headlands on their own peninsula to the east of the Camel estuary. The very high Pentire Point has spectacular views across Padstow Bay and up the Camel estuary, while Rumps Point looks eastwards along the coast and to the offshore rocky islet of The Mouls.

Holywell beach and dunes:
A stunning sandy beach, backed by an extensive and steep dune area, renowned for its wild flowers, including several rare species. Views to seaward include Penhale Point and the rugged twin Gull Rocks.

St Agnes Head:
A high headland with vast views westwards along the coast, and extensive heathland along the headland cliffs and nearby hilltops. Some of the heather here includes the rare Dorset heath, particularly in the nearby Chapel Porth valley. The cliffs are particularly renowned for their tin mining remains, part of the Cornwall and West Devon Mining World Heritage Site.

Top left: Jewel anemones, *Corynactis viridis*, a common inhabitant of rocky reefs.
Image by Paul Naylor.

Top middle: Tompot Blennies, *Parablennius gattorugine*, nestling into a rocky crevice.
Image by Paul Naylor.

Above: A Grey Seal, *Halichoerus grypus*, at close quarters.

Right: A natural granite sculpture on Showery Tor, Bodmin Moor.

Top: Water Mint, *Mentha aquatica*, found in the dampest areas of the Penhale dune slacks.

Above: Round-headed Rampion, *Phyteuma orbiculare*, on cliffs at Marsland Mouth.

13 West Cornwall Coast and Heaths

The final peninsulas

The twin peninsulas of the Lizard and Penwith, linked by the lovely Mount's Bay, are the final tip of southwest England, Lizard Point Britain's most southerly tip, Penwith's Land's End the most southwesterly. Together, they have some of the region's most spectacular coastal landscapes and important wildlife habitats, the coast a series of rugged cliffs, bays and coves, the land a mix of farms and heathland.

Almost the whole of the region is included in the Cornwall AONB, and large parts – particularly the coast – both have SSSI status and are owned by the National Trust. Nearly 20 square kilometres (7.7 square miles) of the Lizard peninsula is protected in a national nature reserve, and two MCZs have recently been established to conserve submarine environments.

Left: The cliffs of Lizard Point, covered with the purple flowers of Sea Aster, *Aster tripolium*.

Above: Marshy grasslands on Goonhilly Downs, part of the Lizard National Nature Reserve.

Above: The cliffs at Kynance Cove.

Below: Croft Pascoe Pool, at the heart of marshy grasslands on Goonhilly Downs, in summer alive with dragonflies and damselflies.

The Lizard's cliffs and heaths

The Lizard is probably most widely known for its spectacular coastal scenery, much of the peninsula lined with rugged rocky cliffs and offshore islets, not only around Lizard Point, but also at such places as Mullion and Kynance Cove.

Inland, the landscape is quite flat and largely treeless, to the untrained eye much of it seeming rather desolate and empty. Yet, the Lizard is enormously important to wildlife conservation. One of the UK's most closely studied natural environments, the peninsula has a hugely diverse plant life, with over 600 species of flowering plants, almost a quarter of the entire UK total! This enormous variety is the result of the mild, wet climate, combined with an unusual and complex geology that together have generated a rich diversity of habitats. Thrown into the mix are the occasional pools that allow marsh and aquatic plants to thrive, plus a few scrub areas, and all this in close proximity to the coastal cliffs with their own very specialised flora.

On the most exposed parts of the cliffs, those rocky areas subjected to salt spray and with little soil covering, the specialised plants that can survive include thrift, sea aster and rock samphire. Further up, where there may be some soil cover, these are likely to include, again thrift and sea aster, but also sea campion, stonecrop, sea carrot and some grasses, such as red fescue and Yorkshire fog. One of the main habitats on the clifftops is maritime heath, covered with ling heather, bell heather and western gorse, as well as such plants as wild thyme, autumn squill and dog violet.

Further inland is found a mixture of wet and dry heaths, particularly on Goonhilly and Predannack Downs. In the damper areas Cornish heath grows

for many years, but eradication of rats from Gugh – one of the birds' main breeding areas – has recently resulted in renewed breeding success. Gugh is also an important breeding site for lesser black-backed gulls, which have a colony spread across grassland and the rocky shoreline at the southern end of the island. Their presence is one of the main reasons behind the SPA designation for this part of the Scillies.

Iconic of all the Scillonian marine birds, however, is the lovely little puffin. Very cute and faintly comical, in the Scillies they breed on Annet and some of the Norrard Rocks, particularly Mincarlo Island. Though it is not possible to land on any of these islands and so get up close to the puffins, they can be readily seen from a boat, either perched on the rocks or swimming just offshore.

Beneath the waves, frequent visitors are dolphins and porpoises, both of which regularly – though unpredictably – pass through Scillonian waters, along with the occasional basking shark and sunfish.

The vast numbers of rocky reefs are home to a huge array of typical species that range from fish such as cod, pollack, bass and wrasse, through crabs, lobsters and starfish, to a host of invertebrates that live attached to the rocks, including pink sea fans, sea anemones, sea squirts and sponges, along with – in the shallower waters – a host of seaweeds that include kelps and many of the well known shoreline wracks.

In a region of great natural beauty, the Isles of Scilly are without any doubt one of southwest England's most beautiful jewels, scene of some of the region's most stunning coastal landscapes, home to some of our most diverse and important wildlife species and habitats.

Above: Razorbills, *Alca torda*, in the Western Rocks.

Above: Puffins, *Fratercula arctica*, on the water near Mincarlo Island, in the Norrard Rocks.

Above: A 'forest' of plumose anemones, *Metridium senile*, attached to a rock at Trenemene, an islet in the Western Rocks.
Image by Paul Naylor.

Places to visit

The Western and Norrard Rocks:
A boat trip out to the exposed western extremities of the Scillies is an absolute must – weather permitting – to see the colonies of grey seals and marine birds.

Tresco:
Worth visiting not only for its lovely Abbey Gardens, but also for its spectacular east coast beaches, particularly Pentle Bay.

Bryher:
Arguably the wildest of the inhabited islands, Bryher's west coast is a rugged series of bays and coves. Head for the appropriately named Hell Bay – its name can only suggest what it must be like at the height of an Atlantic storm.

Outer Head:
The southernmost point on St Mary's, this is a rugged granite headland with some spectacular granite outcrops and boulders.

St Agnes and Gugh:
These twin islands, linked by a sandbar, are the smallest of the inhabited islands, and are home to several species of marine bird.

St Martin's:
The northernmost of the inhabited islands, St Martin's has some wonderful sweeping, sandy beaches, as well as areas of wild moorland.

Far left: A lake shore lined by reeds in the Higher Moors, with farmland behind, St Mary's.

Left: Granite slabs silhouetted against the sunrise, on Peninnis Head, St Mary's.

Below far left: The flower of a Hottentot fig, *Carpobrotus edulis*, in dunes in Pentle Bay, Tresco.

Below left middle: Lousewort, *Pedicularis sylvatica*, on a heather moor, on Gugh.

Bottom left: Rugged rocks along the coast of Annet.

Below: Dunes lining beaches at Skirt Island, Tresco.

Further Information

Here are the websites for a number of relevant conservation organisations, plus many of the protected areas encompassed within *Wild Southwest*.

Governmental bodies

Department for the Environment, Food and Rural Affairs (DEFRA)
www.gov.uk/government/organisations/department-for-environment-food-rural-affairs

Environment Agency
https://www.gov.uk/government/organisations/environment-agency

Joint Nature Conservation Committee (JNCC)
http://jncc.defra.gov.uk

Natural England
www.gov.uk/government/organisations/natural-england

Cornwall Inshore Fisheries and Conservation Authorities (IFCA)
www.cornwall-ifca.gov.uk

Devon and Severn Inshore Fisheries and Conservation Authorities (IFCA)
www.devonandsevernifca.gov.uk

Southern Inshore Fisheries and Conservation Authorities (IFCA)
www.southern-ifca.gov.uk

Non-government organisations (NGOs)

National Trust — www.nationaltrust.org.uk

Royal Society for the Protection of Birds (RSPB) — www.rspb.org.uk

The Wildlife Trusts — www.wildlifetrusts.org

Avon Wildlife Trust — www.avonwildlifetrust.org.uk

Cornwall Wildlife Trust — www.cornwallwildlifetrust.org.uk

Devon Wildlife Trust — www.devonwildlifetrust.org

Dorset Wildlife Trust — www.dorsetwildlifetrust.org.uk

Isles of Scilly Wildlife Trust — www.ios-wildlifetrust.org.uk

Somerset Wildlife Trust — www.somersetwildlife.org

Wildfowl and Wetlands Trust — www.wwt.org.uk

Woodland Trust — www.woodlandtrust.org.uk

Plantlife — www.plantlife.org.uk

The Shark Trust — www.sharktrust.org

Marine Conservation Society — www.mcsuk.org

The British Deer Society — www.bds.org.uk

The Deer Initiative — www.thedeerinitiative.co.uk

Bat Conservation Trust — www.bats.org.uk

British Ornithologists' Union — www.bou.org.uk

British Trust for Ornithology — www.bto.org

Protected Areas

Areas of Outstanding Natural Beauty (AONB) — www.landscapesforlife.org.uk

Blackdown Hills AONB — www.blackdownhillsaonb.org.uk

Cornwall AONB — www.cornwall-aonb.gov.uk

Dorset AONB — www.dorsetaonb.org.uk

Isles of Scilly AONB — www.ios-aonb.info

Mendip Hills AONB — www.mendiphillsaonb.org.uk

North Devon Coast AONB — www.northdevon-aonb.org.uk

Quantocks Hills AONB — www.quantockhills.com

South Devon AONB — www.southdevonaonb.org.uk

Tamar Valley AONB — www.tamarvalley.org.uk

Jurassic Coast World Heritage Site — http://jurassiccoast.org

Dartmoor National Park — www.dartmoor.gov.uk

Exmoor National Park — www.exmoor-nationalpark.gov.uk

Avalon Marshes — www.avalonmarshes.org

Steart Marshes — www.wwt.org.uk/wetland-centres/steart/

North Devon Nature Improvement Area — www.northerndevonnia.org

North Devon Biosphere Reserve — www.northdevonbiosphere.org.uk

Wembury Marine Centre — www.wemburymarinecentre.org

Index